A Kid's Guide to Origami™

Making ORIGAMI BIRDS Step by Step

Michael G. LaFosse

The Rosen Publishing Group's
PowerKids Press™
New York

Dedicated to Miguel A. Martín Monje, of the Asociación Española de Papiroflexia, Spain

Published in 2004 by The Rosen Publishing Group, Inc.
29 East 21st Street, New York, NY 10010

First Edition

Editor: Jannell Khu
Book Design: Emily Muschinske
Layout Design: Michael J. Caroleo

Photo Credits: All photos by Adriana Skura.

LaFosse, Michael G.
Making origami birds step by step / Michael G. LaFosse.— 1st ed.
     v. cm. — (A kid's guide to origami)
Includes bibliographical references and index.
Contents: What is origami? — Duck boat — Duck — Racing penguin — Swallow — Pajarita — Hooting owl — Macaw — Phoenix.
ISBN 0-8239-6702-6 (library binding)
1. Origami—Juvenile literature. 2. Birds in art—Juvenile literature. [1. Origami. 2. Birds in art.] I. Title. II. Series.
TT870 .L234219 2004
736'.982—dc21
                              2002153423

Manufactured in the United States of America

Contents

What Is Origami?

Origami is the art of folding paper to make different shapes. Origami is a Japanese word. *Ori* means "fold" and *kami* means "paper." Although paper folding is not **unique** to Japan, one of the country's most famous origami shapes is a type of bird called the crane. Many Asian peoples consider the crane to be the most beautiful bird in the world. About 500 years ago, one of the first origami books was printed in Japan. An origami crane was included in that book.

With this book, you will learn how to make many types of beautiful origami birds. Most of the origami birds in this book are made from square-shaped paper. You can cut any kind of paper into square shapes. Try using gift-wrapping paper, letter paper, craft paper, or construction paper. If you are using origami paper, make sure you start with the white side facing upward. Experiment with different sizes of paper, too! Drawings help to explain how to fold paper into shapes. No matter which language an origami book is written in, you can learn how to fold any origami shapes by following the drawing instructions and symbols. Study the origami symbols key on page 22 of this book before you begin any of the projects. As you fold, look ahead at the next instruction to see what the paper's shape will look like. This will help you to understand better how the **symbols** and drawings work together. The most important instruction is to have fun!

Duck Boat

This origami model is called the Duck Boat because it is half duck and half boat. It is made to float on water. To prevent your Duck Boat from getting wet, fold it with wax paper. Paper coated with wax is waterproof. You can also color a piece of paper on both sides with crayon to waterproof the paper. Fold neatly so that your duck will balance on water. Open both wings so that the bottom of the duck is wide and flat. Place your Duck Boat on water and make it sail by blowing on it. Have Duck Boat races on the water with your friends.

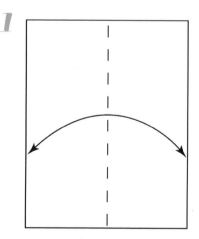

1

Use an 8 ½-by-11-inch (21.6-x-27.9-cm) paper. Valley fold the paper in half lengthwise. Unfold.

2

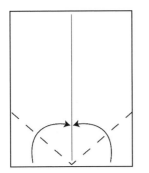

Valley fold the corners of the bottom edge so that they meet at the center crease line.

3

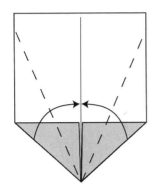

Valley fold the two angled edges of the folded paper to meet the center crease line.

4

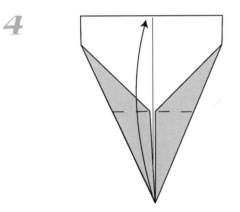

Valley fold up the bottom point so that it meets the middle of the top edge.

5

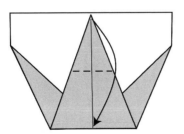

Valley fold down the top point so that it meets the bottom edge.

6

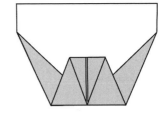

Turn the paper over.

7

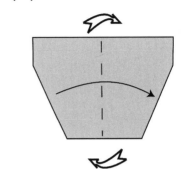

Valley fold the paper in half. Rotate, or turn, the paper to the position shown in step 8.

8

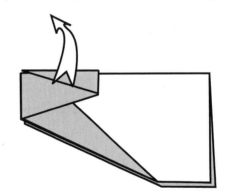

Pull up the neck part of the bird and flatten it to keep it in place. Look below for the shape.

9

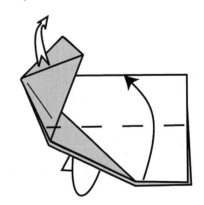

Pull up the beak and flatten it. Valley fold the side facing you to meet the top edge. Mountain fold the other side.

7

Duck

Many **species** of ducks **mate** for life. The mother and father ducks both take care of their ducklings. For these reasons, in many countries, ducks are symbols of family and friendship. They are a common sight in ponds and lakes throughout the world. Ducks that live in public parks are friendly. Many people enjoy feeding the ducks. You can usually tell a male duck from a female duck by its **plumage**. Male ducks are very colorful. The female duck is not as colorful. She can better blend into her surroundings to protect her eggs and ducklings from **predators**.

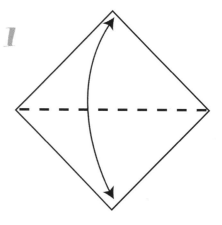

1

Use an 8-inch- (20.3-cm-) square paper. Position the paper so that it is diamond shaped. Valley fold in half. Unfold.

2

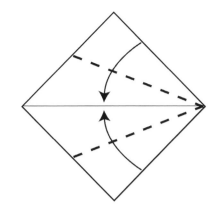

Valley fold the two edges so that they meet at the middle crease.

3

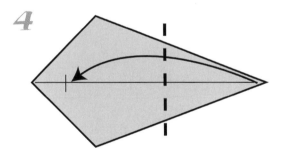

Valley fold the corner to the two corners at the crease line to make a pinch mark. Unfold the corner and turn the paper over.

4

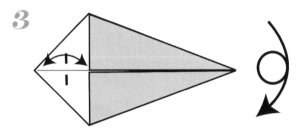

Valley fold the narrow corner of the kite shape to the pinch mark.

5

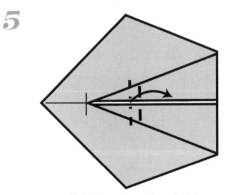

Mountain fold and valley fold to make the beak.

6

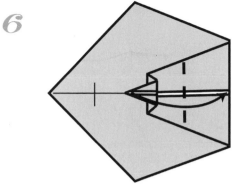

Valley fold the bird's head over so that the beak touches the middle of the folded edge.

7

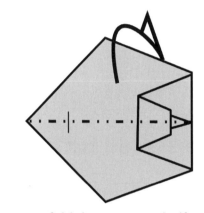

Mountain fold the paper in half.

8

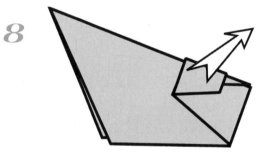

Pull up the neck and flatten it to keep it in place.

9

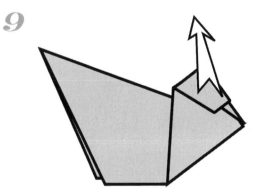

Pull up the head and flatten it.

Racing Penguin

Most penguins live in cold places near or in the **Antarctic**, the area at the South Pole of our planet. The farther you travel from the **equator**, the colder the weather gets. Penguins can't fly to **migrate**, so they rarely live in nature in the **Northern Hemisphere**.

This origami Penguin is designed for racing. You can move the Penguin across a table by blowing on it. Have a Penguin racing contest with your friends. See who can blow his or her Penguin over the edge of the table first. Your origami Penguin will look just like a real one jumping into the water to catch fish!

1

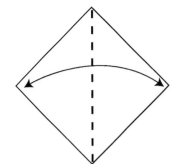

Use an 8-inch- (20.3-cm-) square paper. Valley fold it in half. Unfold.

2

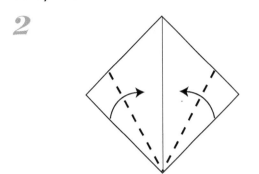

Valley fold the two bottom edges toward, but not all the way to, the center crease to make a kite shape. Look below for the shape.

3

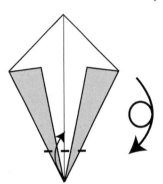

Valley fold the bottom corner. Turn the paper over and position it as shown in the next step.

4

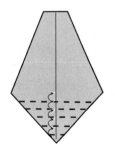

Valley fold the bottom corner five times.

5

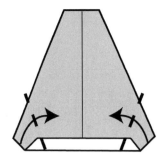

Valley fold the two sides as shown.

6

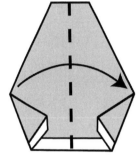

Valley fold the paper in half.

7

Pull up on the beak to make it point forward. Fold up the Penguin's wings on each side.

8

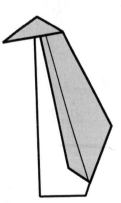

The finished Penguin should stand upright. Blow from the front or the back to make the Penguin move across the table. It works on smooth tables best.

Swallow

This origami bird **represents** the shape of a bird called a swallow. It is based on a **traditional** origami design that can also be used to make butterflies. Swallows are good at catching insects while in flight. Their wings, tail, and body shape help them to change direction quickly in the air to catch **prey**. Swallow origami birds can glide! Fold your Swallow from thin papers for best flight results. You can make **mobiles** by attaching several Swallows to sticks with string. A gentle breeze will move them as if they are in flight.

1

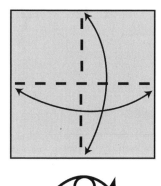

Use a 10-inch- (25.4-cm-) square paper. Valley fold it in half twice as shown to make two crease lines. Unfold. Turn the paper over.

2

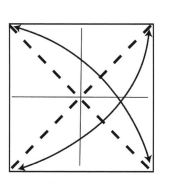

Valley fold the paper in half, corner to corner, each way. Unfold after each fold.

3

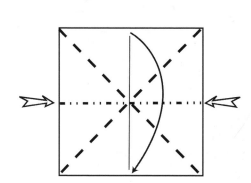

Push in the left and the right edges of the square as you bring the top edge down. Use the creases that you made in steps 1 and 2 to do this. Look ahead to step 4 to see how the shape should look.

4

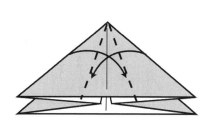

Valley fold the left and the right edges of the top layer triangle so that they overlap evenly. Look at step 5 for the shape.

5

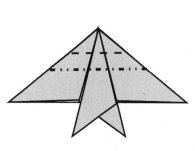

Mountain fold and then valley fold the top corner to make the head.

6

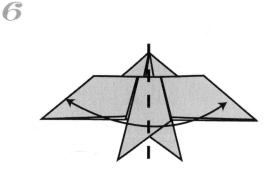

Fold in half, wing to wing, and unfold.

Pajarita

Spain has a rich history of paper folding. *Papiroflexia* is Spanish for "paper folding." The Spanish *Pajarita*, which is sometimes called a little bird or a little parrot, is almost as famous as the Japanese origami crane.

Some people think that the Pajarita looks like a bird. Others think it looks like a horse! However, the Pajarita is regarded as its own character, a little paper pet that anyone can make. This Pajarita is best folded from paper that is colored the same on both sides.

1

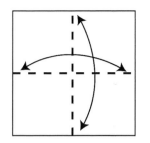

Use a 10-inch- (25.4-cm-) square paper. Fold the paper in half both ways, and unfold.

2

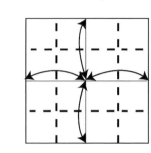

One at a time, valley fold and unfold each of the four edges of the square to the center.

3

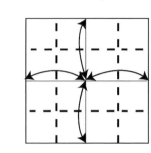

Valley fold the paper in half, corner to corner, each way and unfold. Turn the paper over.

4

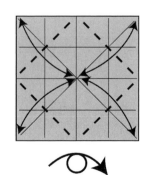

Valley fold each of the four corners of the square to the center. Unfold and turn the paper over.

5

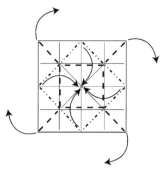

Using the creases that you have made, form a pinwheel shape by pinching each corner in half. The middle edges of the square will meet at the middle of the paper.

6

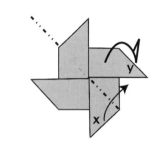

Mountain fold the pinwheel in half. Let X swing up as Y moves to the bottom. Look to step 7 for the shape.

7

Valley fold down the left corner to match the position of the bottom corner labeled Y. Turn the top corner inside-out to make the bird's head. You will need to open up the folded piece temporarily to do the inside-out fold.

8

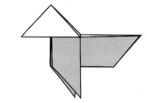

This is the finished shape.

Hooting Owl

Owls are nighttime predators. Owls help people by eating mice, insects, and other pests. For this reason, farmers like to have owls nest in barns or near crops. This origami Owl is an action model. Just pull on the wings, and the beak will rise and fall as if the Owl is hooting! Owls stand for wisdom and learning in many countries because they look so serious and wise. For this reason, origami owls make great bookmarks. This model is an especially clever bookmark. Just hang the Owl's beak over the top edge of the page you are marking.

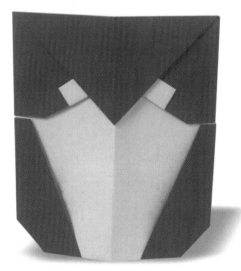

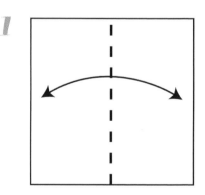

1

Use a 10-inch- (25.4-cm-) square paper. Valley fold it in half. Unfold.

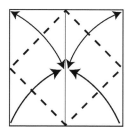

2

Valley fold all four corners to the center crease line. Unfold the top two corners. Look at step 3 to see how the shape should look.

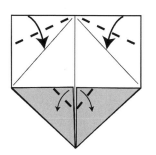

3

Valley fold the right half and the left half of the top edge to the angled creases. On the bottom triangle shapes, fold over the two square corners from the center of the paper. These two corners will be the owl's eyes.

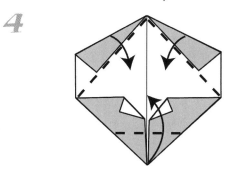

4

Valley fold the bottom corner to cover the eyes partially. Fold over the top folded edges. Use the creases you made in step 1 to do this.

5

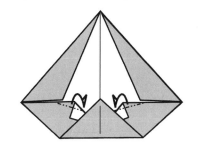

Mountain fold the eye papers to the back as shown. Look at step 6 for the shape.

6

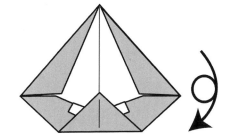

Turn the paper over. Rotate it as shown.

7

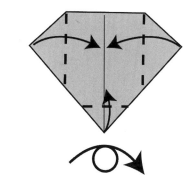

Valley fold the right and the left points to meet in the center. Fold up the bottom point. Turn the paper over.

8

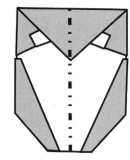

Mountain fold the owl up the center, from the front, so that it can stand on the table like a greeting card.

9

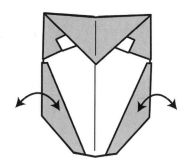

Pull open and close the sides of the owl to make it look as if it is hooting. The beak will move up and down!

Macaw

A macaw is a type of large, **tropical** parrot that is native to Mexico, Central America, and South America. Macaws can live up to 65 years. They are big birds with long, slender tails and large, hooked beaks. Macaws do not make good pets because they are active, large birds. They have powerful beaks, perhaps the most powerful of all the parrot species. They can do serious harm to furniture. However, a paper macaw is perfectly safe! If you use paper that is colored differently on each side, it will add to the beauty of this origami bird.

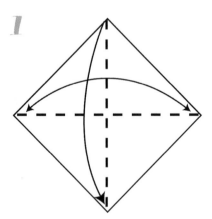

1

Use a 10-inch- (25.4-cm-) square paper. Position the paper so that it is diamond shaped. Valley fold it lengthwise. Unfold. Valley fold top to bottom. Do not unfold.

2

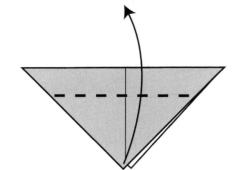

Valley fold the top layer as shown.

3

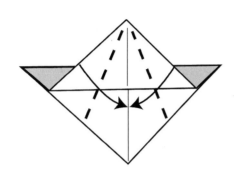

Valley fold the left and the right edges of the top corner to meet at the center crease. Look at step 4 to see how the shape should look.

4

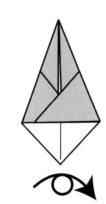

Turn the paper over.

5

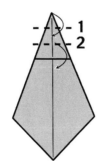

Valley fold down the top corner twice, to the solid line.

6

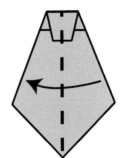

Fold in half lengthwise. Make sure the two wings on either side match up.

7

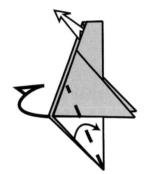

Reach into the top of the paper and pull out the head. Make the tail skinnier by folding the bottom edges on each side to the back edge.

8

Pull down the beak paper. Fold down the top edges of the tail papers on both sides to make the feet.

9

This is how your finished macaw should look.

Phoenix

The phoenix bird has its **origins** in ancient Greek and Egyptian mythology. Mythology is a body of stories that people made up to explain events. The phoenix was said to live for 500 years, burn itself to ashes, rise alive from the ashes, and live for another 500 years. For this reason, the phoenix is a symbol of **eternal** life and **renewal**. The phoenix is said to have the colors of a flame, which are red, yellow, and orange. Use bright, fiery-colored paper to make this origami Phoenix.

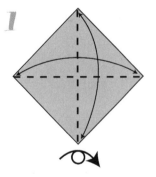

1

Use 10-inch- (25.4-cm-) square paper. Valley fold in half, corner to corner, unfolding after each fold. Turn the paper over.

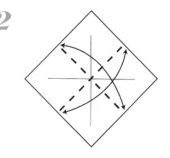

2

Fold the paper in half, edge to edge. Unfold after each fold.

3

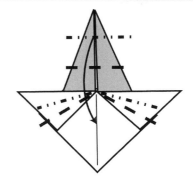

Using the creases, pull down the top corner down to the bottom corner. Push in the side corners so they also come down to the bottom corner. Flatten the shape to make the shape below.

4

Fold the top layer of the bottom left and right edges to meet at the center crease. Unfold.

5

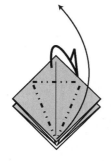

Mountain fold the top corner to the back. Push up the bottom corner of the top layer up to the tip of the arrow as shown.

6

Fold the bottom left and bottom right corners straight out to the sides.

7

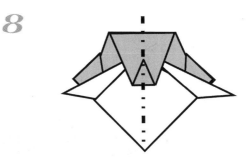

Mountain and valley fold the left and the right points to make fanlike pleats. Mountain and valley fold the top corner to form the neck and the beak.

8

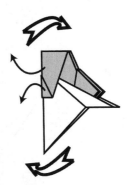

Mountain fold the paper in half, wing to wing.

9

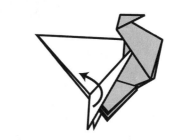

Rotate the paper so that the neck and beak papers are on the top. Pull up the neck, then the beak, as is done in the Duck origami shape at the beginning of this book.

10

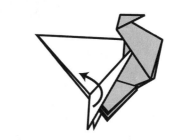

Open the wings.

Origami Key

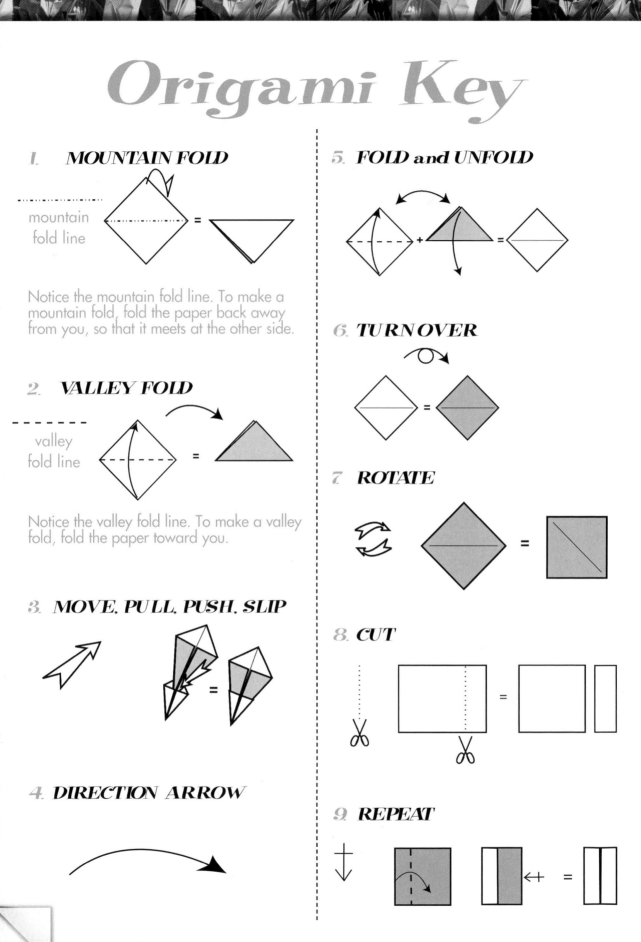

1. MOUNTAIN FOLD

mountain
fold line

Notice the mountain fold line. To make a
mountain fold, fold the paper back away
from you, so that it meets at the other side.

2. VALLEY FOLD

valley
fold line

Notice the valley fold line. To make a valley
fold, fold the paper toward you.

3. MOVE, PULL, PUSH, SLIP

4. DIRECTION ARROW

5. FOLD and UNFOLD

6. TURN OVER

7. ROTATE

8. CUT

9. REPEAT

Glossary

Antarctic (ant-ARK-tihk) The icy, frozen land at the southern end of Earth and the ocean around it.

equator (ih-KWAY-tur) An imaginary line around Earth that separates it into two parts, northern and southern.

eternal (ih-TUR-nul) Lasting forever.

mate (MAYT) To join together to make babies.

migrate (MY-grayt) To move from one place to another.

mobiles (MOH-beelz) Objects, usually with movable parts, that are hung from rods or wires.

Northern Hemisphere (NOR-thurn HEH-muh-sfeer) The northern half of Earth's surface.

origins (OR-ih-jinz) Places where things begin or from which things come.

plumage (PLOO-mij) The feathers of a bird.

predators (PREH-duh-terz) Animals that kill other animals for food.

prey (PRAY) An animal that is hunted by another animal for food.

renewal (re-NOO-ul) To make new or whole again.

represents (reh-prih-ZENTS) Stands for.

species (SPEE-sheez) A single kind of plant or animal.

symbols (SIM-bulz) Objects or designs that stand for something else.

traditional (truh-DIH-shuh-nul) Usual; done in a way that has been passed down over time.

tropical (TRAH-puh-kul) Areas that are warm year-round.

unique (yoo-NEEK) One of a kind.

Index

Web Sites

Due to the changing nature of Internet links, PowerKids Press has developed an online list of Web sites related to the subject of this book. This site is updated regularly. Please use this link to access the list:
www.powerkidslinks.com/kgo/birds/